Making Ice

Checking Your Work

Leona Fowler

COMPUTER SCIENCE For the REAL World™

Rosen Classroom™

It is hot out.

I want to make ice.

How can I make ice?

I put water in a tray.
I put the tray in the freezer.

Will it turn to ice right away?

I wait five minutes.

I check the tray.
It is still water.

I check the tray an hour later.

The water is now ice!

Words to Know

ice

freezer

tray